EXPLORING THE STATES

Missouri

THE SHOW-ME STATE

by Emily Rose Oachs

BELLWETHER MEDIA • MINNEAPOLIS, MN

Note to Librarians, Teachers, and Parents:

Blastoff! Readers are carefully developed by literacy experts and combine standards-based content with developmentally appropriate text.

Level 1 provides the most support through repetition of high-frequency words, light text, predictable sentence patterns, and strong visual support.

Level 2 offers early readers a bit more challenge through varied simple sentences, increased text load, and less repetition of high-frequency words.

Level 3 advances early-fluent readers toward fluency through increased text and concept load, less reliance on visuals, longer sentences, and more literary language.

Level 4 builds reading stamina by providing more text per page, increased use of punctuation, greater variation in sentence patterns, and increasingly challenging vocabulary.

Level 5 encourages children to move from "learning to read" to "reading to learn" by providing even more text, varied writing styles, and less familiar topics.

Whichever book is right for your reader, Blastoff! Readers are the perfect books to build confidence and encourage a love of reading that will last a lifetime!

This edition first published in 2014 by Bellwether Media, Inc.

No part of this publication may be reproduced in whole or in part without written permission of the publisher. For information regarding permission, write to Bellwether Media, Inc., Attention: Permissions Department, 5357 Penn Avenue South, Minneapolis, MN 55419.

Library of Congress Cataloging-in-Publication Data

Oachs, Emily Rose.
Missouri / by Emily Rose Oachs.
     pages cm. – (Blastoff! readers. Exploring the states)
Includes bibliographical references and index.
 Summary: "Developed by literacy experts for students in grades three through seven, this book introduces young readers to the geography and culture of Missouri"–Provided by publisher.
ISBN 978-1-62617-024-7 (hardcover : alk. paper)
1. Missouri–Juvenile literature. I. Title.
F466.3.O227 2014
977.8–dc23
                                                                                2013002366

Printed in the United States of America, North Mankato, MN.

Table of Contents

Where Is Missouri?

Missouri extends over 69,703 square miles (180,530 square kilometers) in the center of the United States. The mighty Mississippi River forms its eastern border. It separates Missouri from Illinois, Kentucky, and Tennessee. Missouri shares its southern border with Arkansas. Oklahoma, Kansas, and Nebraska border Missouri to the west. Iowa is Missouri's northern neighbor.

Jefferson City is Missouri's capital. It stands on the banks of the Missouri River in the middle of the state. The Missouri River snakes across the state from west to east. It joins the Mississippi River near the city of Saint Louis.

fun fact

For over twenty years, Missouri was the westernmost state. It was the starting point for many journeys farther west. This earned the state the nickname "Gateway to the West."

Nebraska

Kansas

Oklahoma

Iowa

Illinois

Did you know?
The Missouri and Mississippi Rivers are the two longest rivers in North America.

Mississippi River

Missouri River

Kansas City

● Independence

● Saint Louis

⭐ **Jefferson City**

Kentucky

● Onondaga Cave State Park

Missouri

● Springfield

Tennessee

Arkansas

N
W E
S

5

History

The Missouri, Quapaw, and Osage tribes of **Native** Americans lived in Missouri when European settlers arrived. In 1803, the United States purchased the Louisiana Territory from the French. The land included present-day Missouri. In 1820, the Missouri Compromise was passed. This deal allowed Missouri to enter the United States as a **slave state**. The following year, Missouri officially became the twenty-fourth state.

fun fact

The state of Missouri was named for the Missouri tribe of Native Americans. *Missouri* means "town of the large canoes."

American explorers meet with Native Americans

Missouri Timeline!

1673: French explorers sail down the Mississippi River. They become the first Europeans to arrive in Missouri.

1803: The United States buys the Louisiana Territory from the French.

1804: Meriwether Lewis and William Clark leave from Saint Louis to explore the United States' new land.

1820: The Missouri Compromise is passed.

1821: Missouri enters the United States as the twenty-fourth state.

1830s: Missouri's Native Americans are forced to follow the Trail of Tears into Indian Territory.

1860: The Pony Express begins to deliver mail between Missouri and California.

1945: Missouri's Harry S. Truman becomes the thirty-third President of the United States.

2011: One of the nation's deadliest tornadoes strikes Joplin, Missouri.

Lewis and Clark

Harry S. Truman

Joplin tornado damage

Mississippi Delta

Did you know?
Missouri is often considered part of Tornado Alley. Most of the tornadoes in the United States happen in this region. Missouri sees between 25 and 30 tornadoes each year.

The Missouri River separates the state into two land regions. The land north of the river is rolling hills and **plains**. Thousands of years ago, **glaciers** covered this region. They left behind rich soil as they slowly moved across the land. Gentle streams wind through the plains.

Missouri's Climate

average °F

spring
Low: 44°
High: 66°

summer
Low: 66°
High: 88°

fall
Low: 46°
High: 68°

winter
Low: 23°
High: 42°

The Ozark Mountains are south of the river. The land is rugged and covered in forests. There are thousands of natural **springs** here. Many produce more than 100 gallons (380 liters) of water each minute. In Missouri's southeast corner, the **fertile** Mississippi **Delta** lies beside the Mississippi River. The southernmost part of this area is called the "Bootheel" because of its shape.

Onondaga Cave
State Park

More than 6,000 caves hide beneath Missouri's surface. Millions of years ago, rainwater seeped into cracks in the earth. The water gradually **eroded** the underground limestone. When the water drained, the caves remained.

Missouri's thousands of caves earned it the nickname "The Cave State." Onondaga Cave State Park is home to some of America's most stunning caves. They are known for their beautiful rock formations. **Stalactites** hang like icicles from the cave ceiling. **Stalagmites** rise from the floor. Marvel Cave is the state's deepest cave. It plunges 383 feet (117 meters) near Branson.

cave salamander

fun fact

Salamanders, bats, and blind crayfish are just some of the animals hidden away in Missouri's caves.

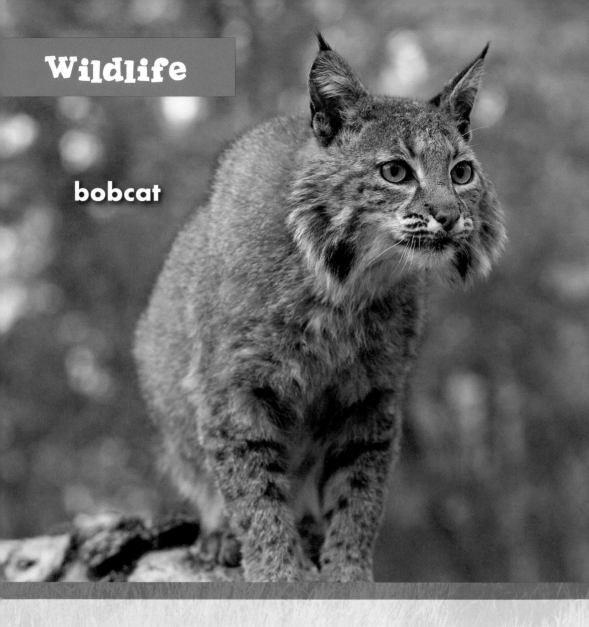

bobcat

Missouri's many parks allow a variety of animals to thrive. Purple martins build their nests south of the Missouri River. Great horned owls and bluebirds roost throughout the state. The **venomous** timber rattlesnake suns itself on rocks. Copperhead snakes settle at forest edges.

copperhead snake

purple martin

great horned owl

Bobcats stalk rabbits in the Ozark forests. Coyotes make their homes on Missouri's grasslands in the north and west. Beavers and river otters live along the state's rivers and streams. White-tailed deer are a common sight in Missouri forests. Raccoons and opossums dwell in both wooded areas and cities.

Landmarks

Missouri is home to many landmarks dedicated to its exciting history. The Jefferson National Expansion Memorial is a park on the banks of the Mississippi River in Saint Louis. The memorial celebrates Missouri's role in **westward expansion**. Here, the Gateway Arch rises 630 feet (192 meters) above the ground. Below the Arch is the Museum of Westward Expansion. It has displays about the history of the American West.

The National **Frontier** Trails Museum is in Independence. It honors the stories of the Santa Fe, California, and Oregon Trails. **Pioneers** followed these routes to settle the West. In Kansas City, the Nelson-Atkins Museum of Art owns over 30,000 works of American, Asian, and European art.

Nelson-Atkins Museum of Art

fun fact

In 1936, Missouri native Thomas Hart Benton painted the walls of Missouri's capitol building in Jefferson City. He was famous for his scenes of the Midwest and American South.

Missouri State Capitol

Saint Louis

16

Saint Louis was built along the Mississippi River just south of where the Missouri River joins it. This has made the city a major transportation center. Many boats stop here with their **cargo**. Saint Louis is one of the country's busiest inland **ports**.

This bustling city also has a rich history. In 1804, Meriwether Lewis and William Clark set out from Saint Louis to explore the Louisiana Territory. In 1834, Missouri slave Dred Scott moved with his owner to a free state. He later went to court in Saint Louis to fight for his freedom. The U.S. Supreme Court ruled against Scott in 1857. This decision began disagreements that would lead to the **Civil War**.

World's Fair 1904

fun fact

In 1904, Saint Louis hosted a World's Fair to celebrate the anniversary of the Louisiana Purchase. To prepare, 1,500 new buildings were built over nearly 2 square miles (5 square kilometers).

Working

Did you know?

The Missouri and Mississippi Rivers give the state over 1,000 miles (1,600 kilometers) of waterways for shipping.

Most Missourians have **service jobs**. They work in shops, restaurants, and hotels. People also work for the government. They have jobs in schools and hospitals. Around two-thirds of Missouri is farmland. Soybeans are the most important crop. Farmers also grow hay and wheat. Some raise cattle and hogs. Turkey farms are common in central Missouri.

Workers in the southeast mine lead, copper, and silver. Oil and natural gas are drilled along the western border. Missourians build transportation equipment such as airplanes, trucks, and boats. They also make chemicals and medicines. The state's location on major waterways makes it easy to ship goods.

Where People Work in Missouri

manufacturing
8%

services
76%

farming and
natural resources
3%

government
13%

Playing

Missouri is home to many popular professional sports teams. Missourians can watch the Kansas City Chiefs or Saint Louis Rams play in the National Football League. In Major League Baseball, fans can cheer for the Kansas City Royals or Saint Louis Cardinals. The Saint Louis Blues play in the National Hockey League.

Missourians water-ski and swim in the state's many lakes. The rivers are perfect for kayaking and canoeing. Fishers head to streams to catch bass and trout. Hunters bring home pheasants, geese, and deer. The Katy Trail attracts bicyclists and hikers. This 200-mile (320-kilometer) path was once a railroad track.

fun fact

Missouri's underground draws many cavers, or people who explore caverns. They use special gear to navigate the caverns.

caving

Saint Louis Cardinals game

Ozark Pudding

Ingredients:

1 egg

3/4 cup sugar

2 tablespoons flour

1 1/4 teaspoon baking powder

1/8 teaspoon salt

1/2 cup chopped nuts

1/2 cup chopped apples

1 teaspoon vanilla

Directions:

1. Preheat the oven to 350°F.

2. In a large bowl, beat egg and sugar until smooth. This may take a few minutes. Stir in flour, baking powder, and salt. Add nuts, apples, and vanilla.

3. Pour batter into a greased pie tin. Bake for 35 minutes.

4. Serve with whipped cream or ice cream.

toasted ravioli

Kansas City is famous for its barbecue. Meat is slow-cooked over burning wood and drizzled in a thick, tangy sauce. Toasted ravioli was invented when a chef in Saint Louis was making fresh ravioli. Instead of boiling them, he accidentally deep-fried them!

In the Ozarks, snow ice cream is an easy dessert to make. People combine milk, sugar, and vanilla with snow until the mixture thickens. Ozark pudding was one of President Truman's favorites. It is made with apples and nuts.

**Lewis and Clark
Heritage Days**

Missourians gather for fun festivities throughout the year. The Rock'n Ribs Barbecue Festival takes place in Springfield each April. Teams from all over the country compete in a barbecuing contest. In May, the Lewis and Clark Heritage Days are held in Saint Charles. Since 1979, people have gathered to celebrate the explorers' westward journey.

Branson's Motorcycle Rally draws people from across the country. Each year, motorcyclists arrive for the music, races, and motorcycle show. In October, around 15,000 people crowd into Trenton for the Missouri Day Festival. It celebrates the state's history with a parade, marching band competition, and arts and crafts market.

Mark Twain

National Tom Sawyer Days

fun fact!

In *The Adventures of Tom Sawyer*, Tom tricks his friends into painting a fence for him. At National Tom Sawyer Days, kids do Tom's work in the Fence Painting Contest!

Samuel Clemens is one of America's great writers. Readers are drawn to his sense of humor. He wrote using the **pen name** "Mark Twain." Clemens was raised in Hannibal, Missouri. His famous novels were set in a similar town. *The Adventures of Tom Sawyer* and *The Adventures of Huckleberry Finn* are about young friends who often get into trouble.

Mark Twain boyhood home

Samuel Clemens

Clemens' popularity lives on in Missouri. His former homes there are now museums. Each year, Hannibal hosts the National Tom Sawyer Days. Many Missourians attend this event to honor Clemens and his books. They appreciate his work and take pride in the state that inspired it.

Fast Facts About Missouri

Missouri's Flag

Missouri's flag has three horizontal stripes of red, white, and blue. The red stands for bravery and the white is for purity. The blue represents justice. A ring in the center of the flag has twenty-four stars. They show that Missouri was the twenty-fourth state. The Missouri coat of arms is inside the ring of stars.

State Flower
white hawthorn blossom

State Nicknames:	The Show-Me State Gateway to the West The Cave State
State Motto:	*Salus Populi Suprema Lex Esto;* "The Welfare of the People Shall Be the Supreme Law"
Year of Statehood:	1821
Capital City:	Jefferson City
Other Major Cities:	Kansas City, Saint Louis, Springfield, Independence
Population:	5,988,927 (2010)
Area:	69,703 square miles (180,530 square kilometers); Missouri is the 21st largest state.
Major Industries:	manufacturing, transportation, services, mining
Natural Resources:	oil, natural gas, lead, copper, silver, zinc
State Government:	163 representatives; 34 senators
Federal Government:	8 representatives; 2 senators
Electoral Votes:	10

State Bird
eastern bluebird

State Animal
Missouri mule

Glossary

cargo—the goods that ships carry from one place to another

Civil War—a war between the northern (Union) and southern (Confederate) states that lasted from 1861 to 1865

delta—the area around the mouth of a river

eroded—wore away

fertile—able to support growth

frontier—an area beyond where most people have settled

glaciers—massive sheets of ice that cover large areas of land

native—originally from a specific place

pen name—a fake name; authors sometimes use pen names instead of their real names.

pioneers—people who are among the first to explore or settle in a place

plains—large areas of flat land

ports—harbors where ships can dock

service jobs—jobs that perform tasks for people or businesses

slave state—a state that allowed slavery; slavery is a system in which certain people are considered property.

springs—pools of water that flow up through cracks in the earth

stalactites—icicle-shaped formations that hang from a cave's ceiling

stalagmites—cone-shaped formations that rise from a cave's floor

venomous—producing a poisonous substance called venom

westward expansion—the movement of settlers to the American West

To Learn More

AT THE LIBRARY

Bodden, Valerie. *Mark Twain.* Minneapolis, Minn.: ABDO Publishing Company, 2013.

Lanier, Wendy. *What Was the Missouri Compromise? And Other Questions About the Struggle Over Slavery.* Minneapolis, Minn.: Lerner Publications, 2012.

Roza, Greg. *Missouri: Past and Present.* New York, N.Y.: Rosen Central, 2010.

ON THE WEB

Learning more about Missouri is as easy as 1, 2, 3.

1. Go to www.factsurfer.com.

2. Enter "Missouri" into the search box.

3. Click the "Surf" button and you will see a list of related Web sites.

With factsurfer.com, finding more information is just a click away.

Index